ALL RI

Cover photo courtesy of Rob Merritt.

Also Available By
Megan Gogerty

<u>*SAVE ME, DOLLY PARTON*</u>

Synopsis: She's read all the books. Bookmarked all the blogs. She should totally have this parenting thing down. So why has she locked herself in her bathroom, the sounds of Dora The Explorer muffled only by her tears? In the follow-up to her smash hit HILLARY CLINTON GOT ME PREGNANT (Named in "Top Ten Plays of 2009" by Atlanta Journal-Constitution), SAVE ME, DOLLY PARTON features Gogerty's quick wit and sharp-eyed takes on politics, pop culture, and parenting. Along the way, chickens are beheaded, people take pies to the face, and various public humiliations are endured. Whether you're a parent or not, a feminist or not, a Dolly Parton fan or not (who's not?), Gogerty will leave you laughing in this comic, freewheeling memoir.

Lady Macbeth and Her Pal, Megan

A solo show

by Megan Gogerty

CHARACTERS

1 W.

MEGAN (W) Forty. A comedian and the author of this show. What a delightful person! Cornfed. Blonde.

SETTING

A mostly bare stage. An actor cube and a ghost light.

Lady Macbeth and Her Pal, Megan was first presented at the Riverside Theatre in Iowa City, IA in February 2017. It was directed by Saffron Henke and starred the author.

Lady Macbeth and Her Pal, Megan

*(A bare stage; a spare acting cube,
nondescript, is carelessly strewn.
There's a ghost light. It doesn't look
magical at all.)*

*(MEGAN, 40, enters with the ener-
gy of an enthusiastic golden retriever.)*

MEGAN

My name is Megan. When people find out I'm

a comedian, like in conversation: "Ohmigod, that

sounds so scary! I could never do that!" and I'm

like, "Aww! I *am* superior!"

I'm *supposed* to feel powerful from it. You get

on stage, you dominate, you kill 'em!

*(Shuffles feet in a non-killing fash-
ion.)*

Lately, I've been a little at sea with it. I feel

restless. I can't sleep. Kinda like I swallowed a

whole walnut.

Oh, let me be clear: I don't actually have any problems. I'm a middle-class white lady with a masters degree. My biggest problem is, "Why don't people love me *even more*?"

But, well - Okay. I had an "incident." One night before a show. It wasn't stage fright, I don't get stage fright. Sometimes I get Stage Concern. But this was different. I got really short of breath, my hands started shaking. Somebody called it a "panic attack," but that seems way overblown. If I could just sleep, I would be fine. It's not like I'm having a midlife crisis. Turning forty was just a coincidence.

The point is, I'm in a slump when find myself having a conversation with my friend Alexis.

Alexis is an actor, and we end up talking about dream roles, parts we'd love to play. And I happen to mention - casually, just throwing it out there - that I think I would make a wonderful Lady Macbeth. And Alexis says:

*(Here, and in other parts of the play
where there are multiple characters, Megan plays all the parts.)*

ALEXIS: *(Derisive snort.)* You can't play Lady
Macbeth.

MEGAN: What do you mean, I can't play Lady
Macbeth? She's a badass, I'm a badass. I could
totally play Lady Macbeth.

ALEXIS: Lady Macbeth is this sexy seductress.

MEGAN: And?

ALEXIS: No, she's this evil… She's carnal.

MEGAN: You don't think I'm carnal? I can be
carnal. I was at a party once in 1998? Carnality
happened.

ALEXIS: It's not personal. Lady Macbeth is not
your type.

MEGAN: I can't believe I'm hearing this. Of course she's my type! It's so obvious. What do we know about Lady Macbeth? She's evil. She's sexy. She's crazy. That's me!

ALEXIS: Megan, Lady Macbeth is a tragic figure of powerful darkness, and you are the human equivalent of a golden retriever.

MEGAN: You don't think I could play Lady Macbeth.

ALEXIS: NOBODY thinks you can play Lady Macbeth!

MEGAN: Well. I am shocked. You of all people, who's supposed to know me so well, can't see…?

(Back to us.) This is what happens to women, we get misconstrued. I blame the movies. Don't even get me started on Cruella DeVil.

Too late! Cruella DeVil is the hero of *101 Dalmatians*! She has a clearly defined life goal. She wants a fur coat. She doesn't kind of want a fur coat, she doesn't want world peace and a fur coat. She wants a fur coat made from puppies. As is her right. She's a bold, competent woman with a poorly conceived business strategy.

(Back to Alexis.)

MEGAN: Just like Lady Macbeth! Alexis! See? I see it! Clear as day! Oh, I could play Lady Macbeth. She is, like, my twin.

Alexis, who has been eating ice cream during all this, dabs the corners of her mouth with a napkin.

ALEXIS: Megan, have you ever read the play *Macbeth*?

MEGAN: *(Scoffing and stalling.)* Look, just because I haven't read something, doesn't mean I can't have opinions on it.

Alexis flicks the napkin in the trash, which is her way of telling me I've lost the argument.

I go home, and - this is the insane part. I can't seem to let it go. Nobody thinks I'm Lady Macbeth? Is it because I'm blonde? Is it because my default resting face is Chipper? *(Demonstrates.)* I acknowledge that my personality may not overtly scream 'Evil Queen.' But I have darkness in me. I'm a woman living in a society that hates women.

That's not fair. We don't hate women. We just don't like them very much? We don't believe them when they tell us things. I wonder if you're going to believe me, telling you this now?

There's a whole stack of studies that proves this.

But see - this is what makes Lady Macbeth so great! She makes sexism work for her! She's a femme fatale, she's Angelina Jolie in every movie she's ever made except the depressing ones about war crimes.

And yeah, she's a murderer. Maybe the guy deserved to get murdered! Maybe he was a bad king. If the system's corrupt, is breaking the law really a crime?

She's so cool: Lady Macbeth in thigh-high boots and a trench coat, smoking a cigarette. She's powerful.

Me, too! I mean: I don't wear thigh-high boots, because they're not practical. But I know a little something about ambition. I mean: look at me. Do you see anybody else on this stage? Clearly, I want to be in charge.

So one day I happen to walk past a bookstore, so I take it home, check it out.

(She reaches into the acting cube - surprise! It's got a lid! - and pulls out a dog-eared paperback copy of Macbeth.)

The Tragedy of Macbeth.

(Opens the book.) Y'all, this play is crazy. If you've never read *Macbeth* - which, by the way, I can't believe you've never read *Macbeth!* - the play is about a lord and his wife who together murder the king of Scotland so he can ascend the throne.

And Lady Macbeth is one of the iconic roles for women in Shakespeare because she actually does stuff. She doesn't just sit around like Ophelia: "Why is Hamlet mad at me?" She's understood to be this total boss.

So it staggers me to discover that she's barely in it. Her husband, Macbeth, has 690 speaking lines, Lady M has 252.

The play opens with the witches, a.k.a. the weird sisters, which savvy audience members will note is also the name of the rock band from *Harry Potter*. Which came first?!

And the sisters are all like, "Hey, Macbeth! We're old and scary! You're gonna be king of Scotland!" So he decides to invite the current king, Duncan, over to his castle.

And that's when we finally meet her: she's reading a letter from Macbeth, and he's telling her about the prophesy and the witches and how the king is coming over, and he calls her "my dearest partner of greatness." Macbeth's a total feminist! So she reads this letter then says to herself:

LADY MACBETH: The raven himself is hoarse

That croaks the fatal entrance of Duncan

Under my battlements. Come, you spirits

That tend on mortal thoughts, unsex me here…"

Unsex me here?

The first time I realized I was a woman, I was eleven years old, studying tap at Charlene's Dance Studio.

Growing up, I love all the old movie musicals. I spend most of my childhood running around in a jauntily-angled fedora.

But now it's time to pick costumes for the recital. Charlene calls a special meeting, students and parents. We have to vote which costume we want, the blue one or the black one. She's taped up pictures of them on the mirror.

They're underwear. Fishnets. Cut to display curves it never occurred to me to worry about not having yet.

And the parents are furious! They can't decide, they love them both! A debate breaks out: Is it better to look like a prostitute from Vegas, or do we want our daughters to be classier, Moulin Rouge-type prostitutes?

I don't know why I'm so surprised - I've seen all those musicals, this is what the chorus girls wear. But somehow I always cast myself in the fedora. You know: the speaking part.

At fourteen, I begin pouring through the teen magazines. I understand now that knowing whether I'm a pear or an apple and how to dress for my shape: these are survival skills. Women should wear high heels because it's more important that a woman's legs appear longer than for her to have the ability to run. It makes sense if you don't think about it.

I'll make it work for me. I'll be the most adorable. I mean, I'm doomed to fail: I have this *(gestures to body)* to work with. I'll never be really… but I'll try. I'll try, and I'll try, and I'll try.

So King Duncan comes to the castle, and it's the night of the murder. They make a big mess, but Lady M says, "a little water clears us of this deed." *(Mimes washing hands.)*

Long story short, they get away with it. Macbeth becomes king, which makes Lady M queen. Mischief managed.

Except that's not the end of the play.

Because Macbeth can't leave it alone. He's all paranoid, so he hires some murderers.

But he doesn't tell Lady M he's doing this. She says, you're acting all twitchy. And he says, Don't you worry your pretty little head about it.

What happened to "dearest partners of greatness"? He becomes king, and she's out with the garbage? Like he could have become king without her!

And she's trying - Trying! - to make this work. She has spent her life surrounded by men, lesser men, murdering their way into glory - it's not like the history of Scotland is all sunshine and democracy. So she said to herself, "Why not me? I'm as good as them."

That's how I felt when I started doing standup - why not me? I was 25, living in Chicago.

Here's what I know about myself at twenty-five: I'm funny. And I have great skin. Everybody tells me so. And I'm too fat. Or disproportionate somehow. I have these hips and this moon-pie face and they're always in my way. I have something in me that I need to get out and I suspect - arrogance! - that other people will want to listen to me. If I could just do it right.

A joke is an elegant piece of rhetoric. Everybody wants to laugh. But you can put a razor blade in the candy apple, you can smuggle all kinds of ideas inside a joke, if you do it right.

The first time I do standup, it's at an open-mic at a bar called the Lyon's Den. I'm the only woman.

The other comics and I view each other askance. They might not have seen a woman before.

I laugh too loudly at the other comics' jokes - courtesy laughs, no one's ever funny at an open-mic - but I'm the only person in the bar doing it. So when I go on stage and tell my terrible jokes, I bring with me the only laugher in the place. It's death.

It's a miracle I ever do it again, but after an eternity of silence, I get my first real laugh. I'm doing a bit about how Christina Aguilera is secretly a member of Mensa but is being forced to sell her body. *[Singing.]* "If you want to be with me, there's a price to pay. I'm a genius in a brothel…"

Getting a laugh on stage…. It's like jumping out of an airplane without a parachute and then discovering you have wings.

It's all I want to do.

Comedy happens in bars, and the bars are full of drunk, leering men. I don't really like being looked at in that way. It makes me nervous. Like my body has accidentally promised something I didn't intend and can't control.

The other comics - some of them will just state baldly that they hate women, all women are liars, bitches, and why can't he get any of 'em to put out? And how he'd like to bend them over, those women, those evil women, bend them over and show 'em. And now here's Megan Something! Try following that with your jokes about Star Trek.

But I keep at it. Like an idiot. It would be different, maybe, if I had one friend who was a comedian. But I can't seem to break into the fraternity.

Most of my friends are poets, musicians. They drink wine and cock their heads: "Why are you doing this?" They don't see the appeal of nightly humiliation.

MEGAN: *(Handing out flyers.)* Comedy show? Comedy show! Wanna see a comedy show?

SOME DUDE: Is it a strip show?

MEGAN: If I were in a strip show, it would be a comedy show.

I head back to the bar.

The headliner comes out of the bathroom. "So it's Joe, then Eddie, then me, right?"

The producer says, "And Megan."

HEADLINER: Oh. You're not gonna talk about your period, are you?

MEGAN: No. Star Trek.

The show starts. My timing's off. The crowd is ugly. It's hard to do comedy from a defensive crouch. The headliner gets up and does twenty minutes that's just crude. They're not even jokes. And the audience rewards him with these hyena barks: "Ha ha ha!"

This is not my room. This is not my kingdom. When am I going to learn they don't want me here? They want me to put on a dress, then take it off again. But first lose ten pounds.

I quit. I retreat into the writing. When you're behind a keyboard, nobody's measuring your waist -to-hip ratio.

Fast forward: I'm thirty-four, living in a small town, teaching theatre to college kids - pardon me, adult learners - when my local theatre company puts out a call for comic monologues. And I happen to have a real humdinger. So I send it in.

PRODUCER: We love it, we want you to do it in the show!

MEGAN: I can't perform it, I'm about to have a baby.

PRODUCER: *(Waving away.)* Aagh! It'll be fine!

So I end up getting onstage, for the first time in a decade, eleven days after giving birth.

From the neck down, everything is swollen. Imagine a Ziplock freezer bag full of mashed potatoes, wearing stretch pants and a V-neck sweater.

But I get out there, I tell my funny story, people laugh, and I have wings.

Maybe I could do it now - comedy.

Once I get started again, I can't seem to stop. I live in a college town that doesn't have its own airport, so I'm clearly not doing it for fame. But the Ziplock bag has freed me. Nobody will look at me that way anymore. Right?

Comedy scenes tend to take on the personalities of their towns. In my small college town, our comics are young, nerdy types who talk about their penis. Then the next town over, there's a lot of factories, so you get more blue collar comics who talk about their penis. There are a handful of women, but mostly it's just fields of penis. It's like the movie *Field of Dreams*, only different. Which: fine. I like men. Men are just like regular people.

I do pretty well in this small little pond. I do very well. And now here I am: queen of my whole backyard.

I should be happy with what I have. Do you know how many people would kill to trade places with me? How dare I ask for more?

Just like Lady Macbeth. She was mistress of Castle Dunsinane - she had a whole castle already! If only she could have been content.

Here's what I know about myself at forty: I'm smart. I may not be the funniest comic in the bar, but I'm the only one who's read Henri Bergson's treatise on laughter, so bring it. I'm goal-oriented. When I die, my tombstone will just say, "Tombstone: Check." I know that the people who told me I was too fat are buying into a narrow Eurocentric beauty standard that is by design impossible to achieve - and anyway, I look great! Although sometimes I catch myself in the mirror, performing surgery on my reflection. I still have excellent skin. Plus I have cheekbones now, gravity is really working for me. I know the world is unkind to women over forty, so if I'm going to say something or do something, I should do it now, right now, yesterday even.

There's a theory that when a woman stands on a stage and talks, that is an empowering act. Look at me! Listen to me for a change! But there's a paradox. The act of standing on a stage invites the audience to objectify. Look at me. Look at this. So a woman on a stage is both empowered and disempowered at the same time.

(Picking up script.) Lady Macbeth: Reading this play was supposed to teach me we have nothing in common, but I see myself in her more than ever.

She's an agitated, ambitious woman conscribed by her circumstances, self-imposed as they may be. She's a firecracker that doesn't have the room to properly go off. I have these images of her stalking the halls of Castle Dunsinane. As I understand, she also had trouble sleeping.

What do the witches think of Lady Macbeth? They never meet. Isn't that odd that the witches are always lurking around on the edges of this play?

Are they invisible? That's the prize you get when you reach menopause, an invisibility cloak.

Macbeth finds them cavorting, being all devilish and supernatural. He goes off to kill some more people, but where's Lady Macbeth?

She's left alone in the castle, where she's having nightmares. She walks the halls, washing the invisible blood off her hands, confessing everything: "Out, damned spot. Out I say! One. Two. Why then, 'tis time to do it. - Hell is murky."

Shut up! Earth to Lady Macbeth! You can't tell people that! One of the first rules of murder and comedy: never admit weakness!

The play ends bloody. Some guy cuts off Macbeth's head and parades it around, and we're supposed to see that as some kind of moral victory.

But before all that... Macbeth is in the castle, waiting for the attack, barking orders.

And then a woman screams. And a servant enters and says, "The queen, my lord, is dead."

And Macbeth... he doesn't ask the obvious question. Somebody comes in, says your wife is dead - what? How?

He knows what she did. She killed. Turned the dagger blade the other way. The ultimate submission.

Is that my fate? Am I looking at a future where my only option besides being objectified is being erased? Because I really think I might be Lady Macbeth, but that's not the compliment I thought it was, it's a death sentence. She's powerless. Does that mean that I...?

I've got to tell you about the panic attack.

I get a call from a booker. There's a world-famous comedian coming through town. Here's how famous he is: people over the age of fifty who don't follow comedy have heard of him. And they want me to open for him.

He's the real deal. Not some ten-cent road comic, this is a real, honest-to-God comedian. A king. Coming to my house. This is my chance to really kill 'em.

Okay. I'm ready. First order of business: I should probably work on my jokes, but I gotta decide what to wear.

I go to my closet - nothing. I go to the mall - nothing. Everything makes me look like I need help buying beer, or else I'm going on a cruise to celebrate my hot flashes.

I can't sleep. Three o'clock in the morning: what do I wear? What do I wear? Do I wear a dress? Skirt? Pants?

I should be working on my material. Don't blow it, Gogerty. Why am I obsessing about this?

Maybe I should just wear all black, just erase this... but then I'm so pale, will I just look like a floating head?

And oh my God, it's the week of the show. I'm having nightmares, what's going to happen? Full-blown panic: this is why I'll never be successful, when the chips are down, I don't have what it takes, I just, I don't know. You want to dress in a way that communicates your comic persona, but who is that? Who am I? And What - What - What do I wear?

And now it's the show, and I wear something, it doesn't matter, I get out there, and now here's Megan Something -

And I choke. Trip on my own knife. And no one to blame but myself.

The headliner is very kind. He's been doing comedy longer than I've been alive. And after-wards, he gives me some advice.

HEADLINER: Your comic persona is not a mask you put on, it's you boiled down to your essence.

MEGAN: How do I know what my essence is?

HEADLINER: What do your friends say about you?

MEGAN: *(Thinking hard.)* I have great skin.

HEADLINER: *(Fondly and sadly.)* Good luck, dear!

Evil, sexy, crazy. Crazy: check.

> *(She takes a hoodie out of the acting cube/box and wraps herself in it.)*

Exhibit B: Sexy.

After my panic attack and subsequent humiliating failure, I think: maybe I'm doing it wrong - comedy. I sign up for this sketch-writing and improv class in Chicago - the big city.

The other people in the class are really...
young. On the first day, somebody says, "Let's
guess how old everybody is." That's how young
they are. Nobody plays that game over 25.

And sure enough: 23, 24, 22, 19. They're
stumped. I have great skin. But I also have a cer-
tain quality. One of them hazards, "I dunno, twenty-five? Twenty-six?" I say, "Close, I'm twenty-
eight!"

It was an impulse. I just knew the word "forty"
would be a splash of acid. I wouldn't be a person
anymore. I'd be their mom. I don't want to be the
mom.

And they buy it! "You don't look 28! You look
younger!" "Ohmigod, I am totally 28, but I don't
feel a day over 27." They laugh, and I'm in.

I spend the next three days being Pretend 28. I love being Pretend 28! It's so much better than Real 28 was. I spent Real 28 being Pretend 39. But Pretend 28: she's a teacher, a substitute teacher! Pretend 28 leaves her hand on your arm just a fraction too long, she's deeply invested in your story, until you bore her. Then she flips her hair and stretches like she's a cat sunning herself on life's great balcony.

They're writing sketches for me where I'm the bombshell. The vamp. This has never happened to me.

I get paired with the oldest a lot - 24. He's not unattractive. For a comedian. He's the airline pilot, I'm the stewardess. He's the cowboy.

He's not unattractive. I mean, he's 24. He's a cable installer who grows magic mushrooms in his apartment.

The last night of the class, we all go out to celebrate. Pretend 28 is holding court, making everybody laugh. After a couple people peel off, 24 leans down - he's very tall and smells like cinnamon - and he whispers in my ear: "I'd be hitting on you a lot harder if it wasn't for that ring."

Of course I didn't take off my wedding ring, why would I, I'm not cruising. I didn't come here for... But it's true I hadn't explicitly brought up my marriage, it never came up in conversation, plus would Pretend 28 be married? I couldn't decide. But he's leaning over me, and and he's very direct.

This has never happened to me before.

"I can walk you to your hotel room. Would you like that?" He's not unattractive. Why don't I say yes? It's not enough that I'm married to my best friend and it would break his heart, I am and it would, but that's not enough of a reason, that's about him, this is about me. This guy doesn't even know my last name. He thinks I'm a substitute teacher. I'm in a strange city, no one would ever know.

My head is buzzing, he smells like cinnamon...

(Blurting.) "I'm not 28. I'm forty. I'm married and have two kids. Here's the youngest, isn't she cute? Here's us on vacation, we rented paddle boats…" *(watches as 24 walks away.)*

Come back! No, don't come back!

Get a grip, Gogerty. It's not like he's the first good-looking person I've ever met. It's that he so clearly desired me. Men desire things and women are supposed to be the Thing That Is Desired, and I have rejected that binary my entire life, one, because it's heteronormative, and two, because I don't want to be that thing on a shelf. But I never knew that being the Thing Desired could feel so...yummy.

And I wasn't even trying! I was in my regulation hoodie and my glasses.

Why have I avoided this feeling for so long? "Oh, Lady Macbeth is a sexy seductress and you're a golden retriever." I'm a golden retriever who knows how to catch a bone! *(High-fives the audience.)*

That's Lady Macbeth's ace in the hole! She's desired, and at the same time, she wants things for herself!

> LADY M: That which hath made them drunk hath made me bold;
> What hath quench'd them hath given me fire.

Of course, she's punished for it. We always punish the women for wanting things. Women are supposed to crab-walk toward their goals: "What, me? No glory for me, please. I'm just grateful for the chance to serve you. If I were to be so fortunate as to earn your respect, or win this election." And if she does get it, she's gotta act like the outcome were a surprise party! Not something that she worked for. "All this for me? You shouldn't have!"

I don't recognize myself. I'm drinking, I'm staying out late. I think inside, the panic attack is still going on.

When I get home, I go to an open-mic two towns over. Pick a table, order a drink. There's a comic on the stage talking about how they should change Shark Week to Vagina Week, because like sharks, vaginas come from below, smell like fish, and to get away from them you punch them in the eye.

And I experience a weird mix of feelings in that moment. My first thought is, Hey, that's actually a joke. It's not a good joke, but he's not just spewing mindless misogyny. He'd worked on this. And my second thought is, vaginas don't have eyes. My third thought is, if I'd heard this joke in my twenties, I would've turned around and never come back. Why put up with it?

But I'm not in my twenties anymore. I'm a grown woman, my body is my own, not a collection of parts to be appraised by some Funyun-eating dill-hole. I get up there and I beat them down. I go supernova: just pummeling them with energy until their eyes melt out of their faces! I kill 'em.

And I step off that stage a mighty warrior in my armor, and the host at the club, some little skid mark, after the show carries on a whole conversation with my breasts: "Hey, girl. You did good up there. You wanna keep doin' good? You want a slot in the show next week? I bet you got a nice slot."

See, I always thought it was me. If I was just funny enough, or clever enough, if I had better clothes, or different clothes, but there's actually nothing I can do to stop it.

Every woman in this room knows what it's like to walk in the dark with your antenna up, to grow eyes on the back of your head, never leave your drink unattended lest someone tries to poison you. To live under threat.

How dare they do that to us - make us live like that?

Lady Macbeth is so sexy. But so what? It doesn't help her. Macbeth becomes king and almost immediately cuts her out. She's gone - from his inner circle, from the play itself. Evil, Sexy, Crazy: Sexy is the only good one, and it gets her nothing. No wonder she goes crazy. To know what you have within you only to be denied! Reduced! Shut out for stupid reasons you can't control! Sexy?! Why don't more women murder?!

Which brings me to exhibit C: Evil.

I'm at the bar one night, me and a bunch of comics. I'm at the bar a lot. One of them's putting together a showcase for new comedians:

COMIC: Hey, Gogerty! Whaddya think of
    Vanessa? Think she's ready to showcase?

Vanessa. She's new. Why are they asking me? I don't know Vanessa. Is it because I'm a woman? Am I supposed to be the expert on all women comedians? I'm feeling sparky. That hungry place where the laughs get mean, where nothing matters but the zinger. Where's it written that I have to like everybody? I'm not the comedy camp counselor.

MEGAN: What do you I think of Vanessa? If she's gonna be that unoriginal, she's gonna need bigger tits.

COMIC: Oohhh! Buuuurn!

The bar erupts. Literal pats on the back! I've joined the fraternity, I'm one of them now. Only cost me a human sacrifice.

I'm on a bender. Open-mic, open-mic, showcase, open-mic. Always the only woman. "Hey, what happened to Vanessa?" Nobody knows. "Doesn't she want to do comedy anymore?" Guess not. I guess she couldn't hack it. Maybe she needs to grow a thicker skin.

Hey, don't be mad at me. I'm a bold, competent woman with a poorly conceived business strategy. And I'm drunk.

I go out to my car without a coat. I'm skidding out on an oil slick of my own self-loathing. Am I doing this to myself, or is it being done to me? This is a nice car. This car could be a weapon. Of course, I left my keys in my coat. My coat made of puppies.

I go back to the bar to get my coat. The show is still going on. But they've added some late arrivals. Two new comics. Bethany and Hannah. Those are women's names. *(Counting.)* One. Two. *(Points to herself.)* Three.

I watch their sets while I sober up. Three women at the open-mic - I can't get over it. The fog lifts.

When there's two women at the open-mic, it's like Thunderdome; there can be only one. But when there's three, we transform back into people again. Maybe three is the magic number. Three's a coven.

(Thunder! Lightning! The
ghost light flickers ominously!)

WITCH: Round about the cauldron go;

In the poison'd entrails throw.

Double, double toil and trouble;

Fire burn, and cauldron bubble.

Here's what we know about the witches: They're wicked. We know this because they're ugly: they're old and have beards and carry toads around.

But what kind of witch are they? Maybe they're Wiccan, I don't know. I don't think I could be a Wiccan, because I don't like to go outside. That seems like it's part of it.

The witches - they've been in this play from the very beginning. It's weird: the witches are the only ones having any fun.

Comedy is supposed to be fun.

A producer calls me up, says "We want you to do a comedy show Saturday afternoon in a furniture store."

I say, "That sounds terrible. I'll do it."

I get there, and it's this high-end, fancy place. Chandeliers. It's like the Vegas of furniture stores.

I screw my courage to the sticking place. And wouldn't you know it, there's a crowd! They got, like, twenty-five people. Which, for a furniture store, is amazing. Everybody reclining in this plush, fine furniture. Sober as a parole board.

And I feel it brewing in me, the panic, the thing I know to be true that I've been shoving away with both hands. I can't make them laugh. I can't make them do anything. I have to make myself.

I have to love them. I have to love them enough to tell them the truth, until they're no longer afraid, I have to tell them, it's okay. I got you. I'm not gonna let you down.

In that furniture store on that Saturday afternoon, I make magic. I have fun, and they have fun, and everybody has wings.

Comedy is not about killing. It's about turning a group of individuals into a crowd, it's about stoking that crowd into waves of ecstasy. Comedy is sex. But not in the fishnet way, but in the way of the crones dancing naked around the maypole. In the way of the seasons and the solstice.

I don't have to be Lady Macbeth. I have another option. The thing that saves me from her fate is that Lady Macbeth can't make a joke.

MEGAN: Hey, Alexis! I think I might be a witch!

ALEXIS: Obviously. You think I need somebody to tell me that my best friend is magical? I could've told you that, you stupid idiot.

Alexis insults people when she loves them. I make them characters in my plays. Friendship!

Poor Lady Macbeth. Trapped in that terrible story. She doesn't even have a friend.

(Dawning.) Yes, she does. She has me. I can be her best friend, her gal pal. I have magic powers. I can rewrite the play.

Let's say when she first gets the letter from her husband telling her about the prophesy, let's say she doesn't call down the spirits who tend on mortal thoughts. Let's say she goes out.

> *(The hoodie Megan wears transforms magically into a glorious, floor-length, hooded cape. It's magic.)*

Let's say she strikes out into the Scottish Highlands, poking through the moors and outcroppings until she finds them herself, stroking their beards and calling down the goddess.

She would ask them:

LADY MACBETH: Why corrupt my husband?

And they would cackle and say,

WITCH: We simply expose the truth. That hard, little walnut you've swallowed - you think that can be eased by being crowned a queen? That kernel, that hunger, is the life force. That is our call. You will join us in the circle. We will dance naked in the moonlight, clutch hands, and then you will know what it truly means to fly!

A joke is magic. If Lady Macbeth could make a joke... Maybe then she'd have a first name. She could go to a Scottish open-mic. *(Terrible brogue:)* "Put your hands together for Connie Macbeth!"

She could be like, *(terrible brogue:)* "My husband the king is so tyrannical, if he were a dinosaur, he'd be a Tyrannosaurus Rex!"

I don't know what's worse, that joke or my accent.

There's a superstition that if you say the name of the Scottish Play in a theatre, you'll be cursed. I don't believe it. That idea implies that evil is outside of you. Witch, please.

However, we have brought her forth. And she has been so misused. She deserves, if not forgiveness, then respect. Love.

We need three: I'm one, she's the second. You're third. Welcome to the coven.

> *(Megan takes off the cape and spreads it out, making an alter cloth. Kneels. Begins to cast a spell.)*

Goddess of Comedy! Because obviously you're a woman.

Y'know what, I need a wand - *(rummages in the box, pulls out a rubber chicken.)*

Goddess of Comedy!

Release our friend Connie Macbeth! She was gonna keep her maiden name, but, her husband wanted to go into politics.

She killed herself, Goddess. Whether she was defeated by the world or else she sabotaged herself, but either way, she thought it was her only option. But Goddess, I would like to believe there exists a space in our collective imagination where she lives on. A place where she can grow old and laugh, is not held hostage by the violent hierarchies of kings and queens.

Empower her, Goddess! And by empowering her, you embolden us all! For we are still here, walking this earth, and we are all Connie Macbeth. And they want us to buy into their hoodwink. But

Goddess, you can teach us to play our own games.

You can give us magic!

I wish you jokes. And sex. The good kind.

May the truth set us free. Blessed be.

(Blows a kiss. Darkness.)

END OF PLAY.

Also By Megan Gogerty

BAD PANDA

Synopsis: They're the last two pandas on earth. It's mating season. One of them falls in love with a crocodile. Who is gay. And then the baby comes. In this sweet celebration of non-traditional families, Gwo Gwo the panda must balance his newfound desire for Chester the crocodile with his obligations to his prescribed panda mate, Marion. The animals eat, mate, splash around in identity politics, wrestle with the ambivalence of parenthood, and love one another as only families can.

Cast Size: 2 Males, 1 Female

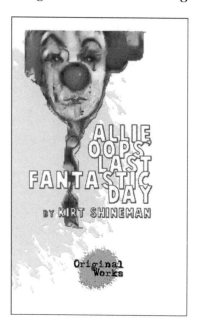

ALLIE OOPS' LAST FANTASTIC DAY
by Kirt Shineman

Synopsis: While Sue, a mother, waits for the doctor to call for oncology results, she prepares for her son's last year of high school. As is their tradition, Sue attends the first day of school as a clown, Allie Oop, to bring in the new year, but this year, this day, is not as fantastic as she would hope. With the help of her humor and bag of tricks she fools even the toughest foe.

Cast Size: 1 Female

COMMENCEMENT
by Clay McLeod Chapman

Synopsis: One actress plays three women drawn together in the grim aftermath of a high school shooting - the mother of the shooter (staph infection), one of the shooter's victims (early release), and the mother of that victim (keynote speaker). It is a deep exploration of the lives of three women that, according to SEE Magazine "... will leave you wringing your hands in helpless empathy."

Cast Size: 1 Female (may be produced with 3 Females)